Fact Finders™

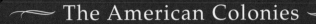

The American Colonies

The South Carolina Colony

by Susan E. Haberle

Consultant:
Paul A. Horne, Jr.
Executive Director
South Carolina Council for the Social Studies

Mankato, Minnesota

Fact Finders is published by Capstone Press,
151 Good Counsel Drive, P.O. Box 669, Mankato, Minnesota 56002.
www.capstonepress.com

Library of Congress Cataloging-in-Publication Data
Haberle, Susan E.
   The South Carolina colony / by Susan E. Haberle.
   p. cm.—(Fact Finders. The American colonies)
   Includes bibliographical references and index.
   ISBN 0-7368-2683-1 (hardcover)
   1. South Carolina—History—Colonial period, ca. 1600–1775—Juvenile literature.
I. Title. II. Series: American colonies (Capstone Press)
F272.H33 2006
975.7'02—dc22   2004029505

Summary: An introduction to the history, government, economy, resources, and people of
   the South Carolina Colony. Includes maps and charts.

Editorial Credits
Katy Kudela, editor; Jennifer Bergstrom, set designer, illustrator, and book designer;
   Bobbi J. Dey, book designer; Wanda Winch, photo researcher/photo editor

Photo Credits
Cover image: A view of Charles Town, the capital of South Carolina in 1767,
   The Mariners' Museum

Corbis/Historical Picture Archive, 4–5
Getty Images Inc./MPI, 9
The Granger Collection, New York, 10, 18, 20–21, 22
Mary Evans Picture Library, 11, 19
North Wind Picture Archives, 8, 12–13, 16–17, 26–27, 29 (both)
Rick Reeves, 15

1 2 3 4 5 6 10 09 0

Table of Contents

~ Chapter 1 ~
South Carolina's First People

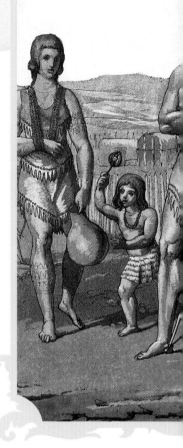

Long before Europeans came, American Indians lived in what is now South Carolina. The two largest groups were the Cherokee and the Catawba.

The two groups settled in different areas of South Carolina. The Cherokee lived in the Appalachian Mountains. The Catawba lived in the **foothills**. Both groups used materials from the nearby forests to build their homes. They built houses of logs and tree bark.

The Yamassee Indians lived south of the Appalachian Mountains. Their homes were built with wooden poles covered with leaves from **palmetto** trees.

American Indians in South Carolina used bows and arrows to hunt wild game.

For food, South Carolina Indians hunted deer and wild turkeys. They also gathered nuts and berries. Some Indians grew corn, beans, and squash.

Chapter 2

Early Settlers

During the 1500s, Spanish and French explorers each tried to settle in South Carolina. The food they raised didn't last through the winter. Many of the explorers fought with each other. Some died from diseases. When their settlements failed, they sailed back to Europe.

England Claims Land

In 1629, King Charles I of England decided to start a new colony. The king **granted** a strip of land to Sir Robert Heath. Heath's land was in North Carolina and South Carolina. King Charles I named the colony Carolana.

South Carolina was once part of a larger colony called Carolana. South Carolina's final borders were set in 1763. ➡

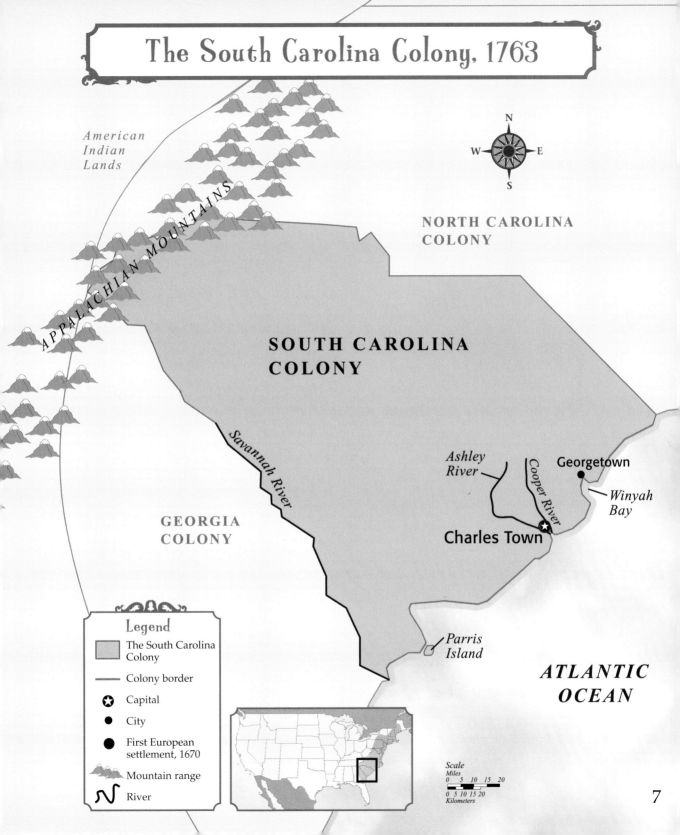

The South Carolina Colony, 1763

American Indian Lands

APPALACHIAN MOUNTAINS

NORTH CAROLINA COLONY

SOUTH CAROLINA COLONY

GEORGIA COLONY

Savannah River

Ashley River

Cooper River

Georgetown

Winyah Bay

Charles Town

Parris Island

ATLANTIC OCEAN

N
W E
S

Legend

The South Carolina Colony

Colony border

★ Capital

● City

● First European settlement, 1670

Mountain range

River

Scale
Miles
0   5   10 15 20

0 5 10 15 20
Kilometers

King Charles II of England granted Carolina's land to the Lords Proprietors.

Sir Heath's plans for the land in North America did not develop. There were no settlements built.

In 1663, King Charles II of England granted the same land to eight Englishmen. This group of men was called the Lords Proprietors. They stayed in England and appointed governors to rule the colony in North America.

The colony's name changed to Carolina. King Charles II also added more land. The Carolina colony included land in the present-day states of North Carolina, South Carolina, Georgia, and Florida.

Early Settlement

The Lords Proprietors sent a group of settlers to Carolina. Some of the settlers came from England. Others came from an English colony on the island of Barbados.

In March 1670, the group of settlers founded Charles Town. Its location near two rivers and the Atlantic Ocean allowed settlers to ship goods to Europe. The rivers also provided water for crops.

Settlers arriving in the Carolina Colony found American Indians settled on the land. ▼

9

In 1712, the Lords Proprietors decided to manage the colony separately. They split the land into North and South Carolina.

The English settlements changed life for the American Indians. They had to share their land. Some English traders also treated the Indians unfairly. The Yamassee Indians became angry. They fought the colonists in the Yamassee War (1715–1716).

Many colonists and Indians were killed during the Yamassee War.

After the war, the Yamassee were forced to leave. They moved south of the Savannah River into what is now Georgia.

Despite the extra land gained from the war, settlement in South Carolina was slow. People feared more Indian attacks.

During the mid-1700s, word spread about the good farmland in South Carolina. Settlers began to move from northern colonies to South Carolina.

As more people settled in South Carolina, Charles Town grew into a busy seaport.

Chapter 3

Colonial Life

South Carolina's varied land led to the growth of two separate areas in the colony. Daily life was different in each area.

The mountains and foothills were called the Up Country. There, farmers lived in log cabins. They owned few belongings. People slept on mattresses made of pine branches. They covered the dirt floors of their cabins with pine needles.

Farms in the Up Country were small. Settlers grew corn, melons, squash, and beans for their families. They hunted deer and bears. They also raised pigs, cattle, chickens, and turkeys.

Some colonists settled in the mountains of South Carolina.

13

South Carolina Colony's Exports

Agricultural Exports
indigo
rice

Industrial Exports
furniture
ships

Natural Resource Export
lumber

Many wealthy colonists lived in the Low Country area near the coast. They grew rice, **indigo,** and other crops on large farms called **plantations**. They lived in large brick houses with gardens.

Pirates Along the Coast

People who lived in the Low Country faced danger from pirates. Pirates tried to block ships from sailing into Charles Town's harbor. They stole goods that the ships had carried from Europe.

Blackbeard was a famous colonial pirate. He and his crew were a threat to the colony. In 1718, Blackbeard took control of Charles Town's harbor. He did not leave the city until he had medicine for his sick crew.

Education

Schools were not widespread in the southern colonies. The few schools were built in larger cities. Most South Carolina colonists could not afford to send their children to school. Wealthy colonists hired tutors to teach their children.

Blackbeard and his pirate crew often stole from ships bringing goods to South Carolina. ➡

15

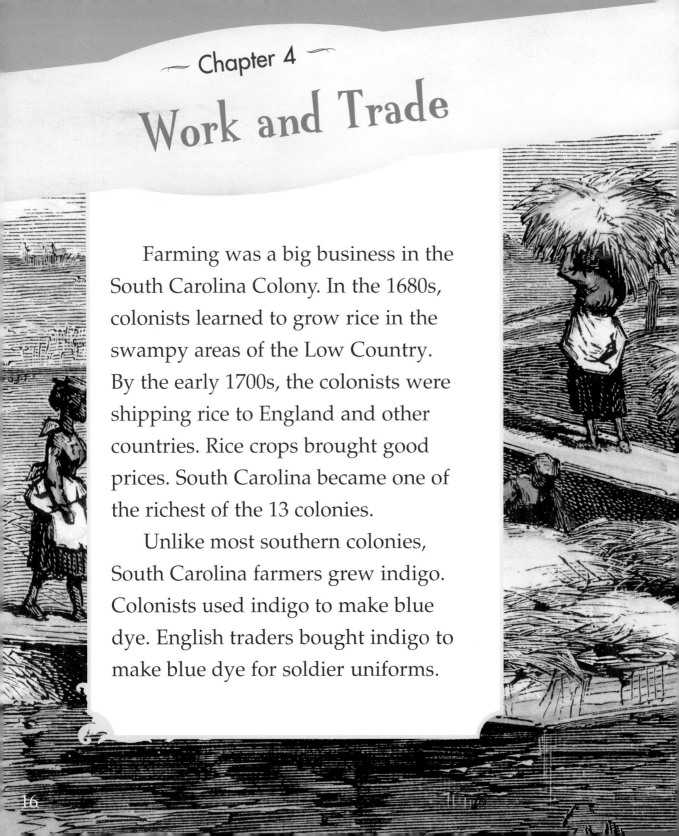

Chapter 4

Work and Trade

Farming was a big business in the South Carolina Colony. In the 1680s, colonists learned to grow rice in the swampy areas of the Low Country. By the early 1700s, the colonists were shipping rice to England and other countries. Rice crops brought good prices. South Carolina became one of the richest of the 13 colonies.

Unlike most southern colonies, South Carolina farmers grew indigo. Colonists used indigo to make blue dye. English traders bought indigo to make blue dye for soldier uniforms.

Slaves helped transport
South Carolina's rice crops.

17

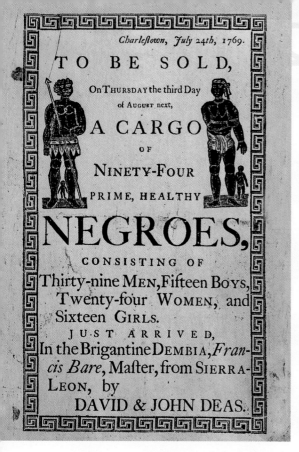

Posters advertised the sale of slaves in Charles Town, South Carolina.

FACT!

Rice was valuable in the South Carolina Colony. By 1690, South Carolina colonists could pay their taxes with rice.

Slave Labor

Growing rice and indigo took a lot of work. The colony's plantations needed many workers. Some plantation owners forced American Indians to work as slaves. Other plantation owners bought slaves from Africa and the West Indies. Many slaves knew how to grow rice and indigo.

Coastal Industries

Some colonists fished along South Carolina's coastal islands. Fishers caught oysters, clams, and shrimp from the ocean.

Other colonists fished from South Carolina's many streams and rivers. They caught bass and trout.

As South Carolina grew, so did its shipbuilding businesses. Between 1735 and 1775, colonists built more than 300 wooden ships. Colonists also made shipbuilding supplies from cypress and pine trees. Shipbuilding was the colony's largest industry.

Shipbuilders had a lot of business in South Carolina. ▼

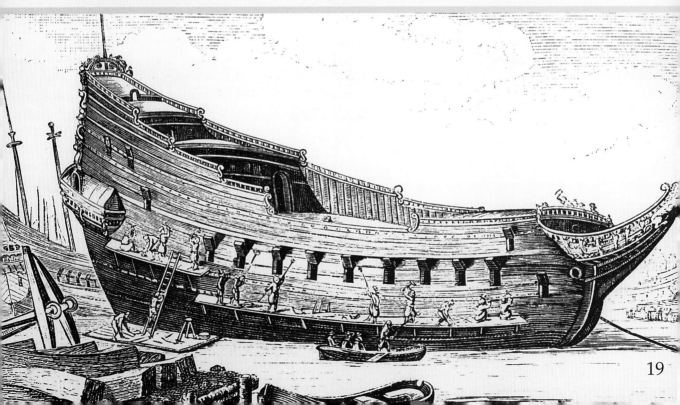

Chapter 5

Community and Faith

South Carolina grew into a rich colony. Most of the wealth came from the Low Country. There, plantation owners bought slaves. The added help meant larger crops and more money.

In the Up Country, colonists lived differently. They worked as small farmers and traders. They did not buy many slaves.

Slave Community

The Low Country's demand for slaves changed South Carolina. By 1720, more slaves than colonists lived in the colony.

Slaves had poor living conditions. Although slaves were unhappy, there were only a few uprisings in the colonies.

Slave auctions took place in South Carolina even after the colony became a state. This painting shows a slave auction in the 1800s.

NEGROES
FOR SALE
AT AUCTION
THIS DAY
AT 1 O'CLOCK

NOTICE

The first uprising took place in South Carolina. In 1739, a group of slaves stole guns from a store near Charles Town. Both slaves and colonists died.

Religious Groups

South Carolina's farmland brought more than wealth. The land attracted people from other colonies.

Quakers traveled into town to worship. They gathered to pray at a meetinghouse. ⬇

The new settlers came from many religious groups. The **Quakers** came from Pennsylvania and Virginia to farm new land. Some Baptists moved from the New England colonies.

People of many other faiths settled on South Carolina's land. Lutherans, Jews, and French **Huguenots** came from Europe. They found the religious freedom they wanted in South Carolina.

Population Growth of the South Carolina Colony

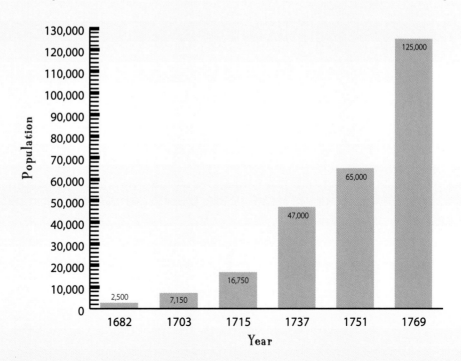

Chapter 6

Becoming a State

By the mid-1700s, many colonists wanted independence from Great Britain. They did not like being controlled by British rulers. Some colonists in South Carolina were angry with the British laws that limited colonial trade. Many were also tired of paying taxes to Great Britain.

Representatives from the colonies formed the Continental Congress. They met to discuss the troubles with Great Britain. In July 1776, members of Congress approved the Declaration of Independence. This document declared the colonies free of British rule. But the colonists had to fight for independence.

South Carolina was part of the Southern Colonies. ➡

The Thirteen Colonies, 1763

Claimed by
**NEW YORK COLONY and
NEW HAMPSHIRE COLONY**

**NEW
HAMPSHIRE
COLONY**

**NEW YORK
COLONY**

**MASSACHUSETTS BAY
COLONY**

**PENNSYLVANIA
COLONY**

**RHODE ISLAND
COLONY**

**CONNECTICUT
COLONY**

**NEW
JERSEY
COLONY**

**DELAWARE
COLONY**

**VIRGINIA
COLONY**

**MARYLAND
COLONY**

**NORTH
CAROLINA
COLONY**

*ATLANTIC
OCEAN*

**SOUTH
CAROLINA
COLONY**

N
W   E
S

**GEORGIA
COLONY**

Scale
Miles
0   30   60   90 120

0   60   120
Kilometers

Legend

New England Colonies

Middle Colonies

Southern Colonies

Present-day States

Fight for Freedom

The colonists' fight for freedom lasted eight years. During the Revolutionary War (1775–1783), nearly 200 battles were fought in South Carolina.

Not all of the battles were fought against Britain. People in the Up Country were angry with Charles Town's leaders. Many were loyal to the British. People in the Low Country wanted freedom. Colonists often raided the homes of those who disagreed with them.

Colonists won the Battle of Kings Mountain in a little more than an hour. The battle in South Carolina kept the British from advancing north.

The American colonists won the war in 1783. They gained their freedom from Great Britain.

In 1787, members of Congress decided to create a stronger government. The **Constitution** of the United States brought the states together under a powerful national government.

On May 23, 1788, South Carolina's legislature approved the Constitution. South Carolina became the eighth state to join the United States.

FACT!

Charles Town was renamed Charleston in 1783 to make it sound less British.

Fast Facts

Name
The South Carolina Colony

Location
Southern colonies

Year of Founding
1670

First Settlement
Charles Town

Colony's Founders
Lords Proprietors

Religious Faiths
Baptist, Church of England, Episcopalian, French Huguenot, Jewish, Lutheran, Quaker

Agricultural Products
Indigo, rice

Major Industries
Fishing, shipbuilding

Population in 1769
125,000 people

Statehood
May 23, 1788
(8th state)

Time Line

1663
King Charles II of England grants more land; he gives the colony to the Lords Proprietors.

1629
King Charles I of England grants land that is now North Carolina and South Carolina.

1500s
Explorers from Spain and France try and fail to build permanent settlements in South Carolina.

1712
North Carolina and South Carolina split into two separate colonies.

1707
An Act of Union unites England, Wales, and Scotland; they become the Kingdom of Great Britain.

1670
Charles Town becomes South Carolina Colony's first settlement.

1763
Proclamation of 1763 sets colonial borders and provides land for American Indians.

1775-1783
American colonies fight for their independence from Great Britain in the Revolutionary War.

1776
Declaration of Independence is approved in July.

1788
On May 23, South Carolina is the eighth state to join the United States.

Glossary

constitution (kon-stuh-TOO-shuhn)—the written system of laws in a state or country that state the rights of the people and the powers of the government

foothill (FUT-hil)—a low hill at the base of a mountain

grant (GRANT)—a gift such as land or money given for a particular purpose

Huguenot (HYOO-guh-nawt)—a French non-Catholic of the 16th and 17th centuries

indigo (IN-duh-goh)—a plant that has dark purple berries that can be made into dye

palmetto (pal-MET-oh)—a type of palm tree

plantation (plan-TAY-shuhn)—a large farm where crops such as indigo and rice are grown

Quaker (KWAY-kur)—a member of the Religious Society of Friends, a religious group founded in the 1600s, that prefers simple religious services and opposes war

Internet Sites

FactHound offers a safe, fun way to find Internet sites related to this book. All of the sites on FactHound have been researched by our staff.

Here's how:

1. Visit *www.facthound.com*
2. Type in this special code **0736826831** for age-appropriate sites. Or enter a search word related to this book for a more general search.
3. Click on the **Fetch It** button.

FactHound will fetch the best sites for you!

Read More

Blashfield, Jean F. *The South Carolina Colony.* Our Thirteen Colonies. Chanhassen, Minn.: Child's World, 2004.

Horne, Paul A. Jr., and Patricia H. Klein. *South Carolina: The History of an American State.* Selma, Ala.: Clairmont Press, 2000.

Krebs, Laurie. *A Day In The Life of a Colonial Indigo Planter.* The Library of Living and Working in Colonial Times. New York: PowerKids Press, 2004.

Index